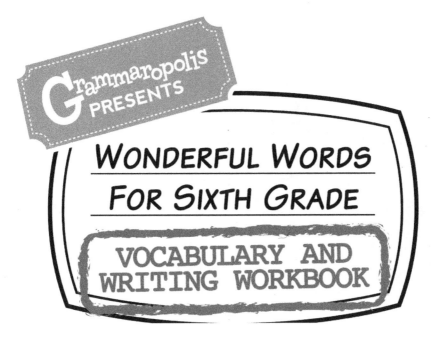

Grammaropolis
PRESENTS

WONDERFUL WORDS
FOR SIXTH GRADE

VOCABULARY AND WRITING WORKBOOK

BY ORDER OF

The Mayor of Grammaropolis

Written by Christopher Knight
Interior Design by Christopher Knight
Cover Design by Mckee Frazior
Grammaropolis Character Design by Powerhouse Animation & Mckee Frazior

ISBN: 9781644420560
Copyright © 2021 by Grammaropolis LLC
All rights reserved.
Published by Six Foot Press
Printed in the U.S.A.

Grammaropolis.com
SixFootPress.com

Grammaropolis PRESENTS

WONDERFUL WORDS
FOR SIXTH GRADE

VOCABULARY AND
WRITING WORKBOOK

GRAMMAROPOLIS BOOKS

HOUSTON

FROM THE DESK OF THE MAYOR

Greetings, fellow wordsmith!

Thank you so much for using this workbook. I hope you have fun learning some new vocabulary words!

As you know, many words can act as multiple parts of speech; it all depends on how they're used in the sentence. For the sake of clarity and simplicity (and because we didn't have enough space on the page!), the definitions in this workbook include only one part of speech for each word.

It's great to know a lot of vocabulary words, but the real reason we expand our vocabulary is so that we can communicate more effectively. That's why I've added a writing exercise, with optional prompts, at the end of each section.

Thanks again for visiting Grammaropolis. I hope you enjoy your stay!

—The Mayor

TABLE OF CONTENTS

HOW TO USE THE VOCABULARY PAGES

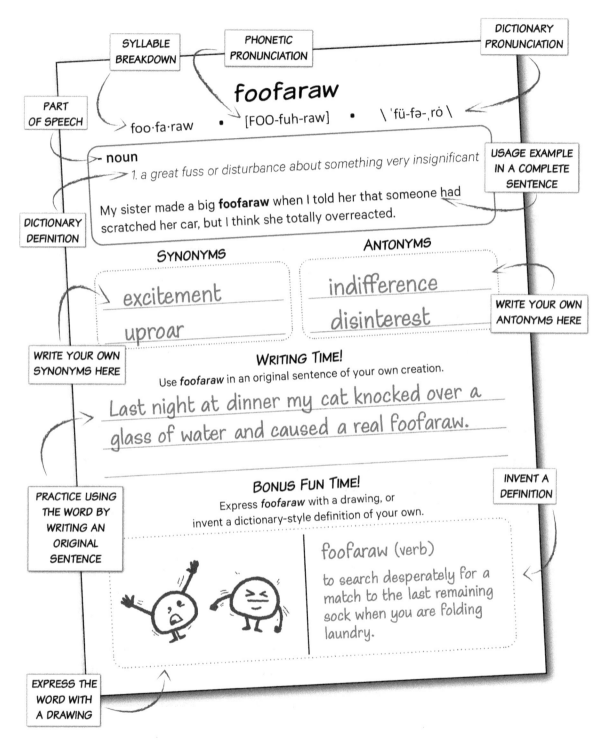

SYLLABLE BREAKDOWN

PHONETIC PRONUNCIATION

DICTIONARY PRONUNCIATION

foofaraw

foo·fa·raw • [FOO-fuh-raw] • \ ˈfü-fə-ˌrȯ \

PART OF SPEECH

noun

1. a great fuss or disturbance about something very insignificant

USAGE EXAMPLE IN A COMPLETE SENTENCE

My sister made a big **foofaraw** when I told her that someone had scratched her car, but I think she totally overreacted.

DICTIONARY DEFINITION

SYNONYMS

excitement

uproar

ANTONYMS

indifference

disinterest

WRITE YOUR OWN ANTONYMS HERE

WRITE YOUR OWN SYNONYMS HERE

WRITING TIME!

Use *foofaraw* in an original sentence of your own creation.

Last night at dinner my cat knocked over a glass of water and caused a real foofaraw.

PRACTICE USING THE WORD BY WRITING AN ORIGINAL SENTENCE

BONUS FUN TIME!

Express *foofaraw* with a drawing, or invent a dictionary-style definition of your own.

INVENT A DEFINITION

foofaraw (verb)

to search desperately for a match to the last remaining sock when you are folding laundry.

EXPRESS THE WORD WITH A DRAWING

Important Note: Synonyms and antonyms for nouns might be harder to come up with than they are for verbs and adjectives, but do your best!

THE PARTS OF SPEECH REVIEW

Every word acts as at least one of the eight parts of speech. In this workbook, you'll find nouns, verbs, and adjectives. Here are some things you need to remember about them!

NOUNS
A noun can name a person, place, thing, or idea.

Naming a person:
Jason is my very best **friend**.

Naming a place:
Becks Prime is my favorite **restaurant**.

Naming a thing:
That **ball** is my favorite **toy**.

Naming an idea:
Honesty and **loyalty** are my best **qualities**.

VERBS
An action verb expresses mental or physical action, and a linking verb expresses a state of being.

Expressing physical action:
Richard **jumped** across the river.

Expressing mental action:
Richard **considered** jumping across the river.

Expressing a state of being:
Richard **feels** bad. He **is** sorry for jumping across the river.

ADJECTIVES
*An adjective modifies a noun or a pronoun and tells **what kind, which one, how much,** or **how many**.*

Modifying a noun:
The **quick brown** fox jumped over the **enormous red** fence at the **first** sign of trouble.

Modifying a pronoun:
They are **satisfied** with the answer, but I am still **curious**.

There are five other parts of speech you won't find in this workbook, but that doesn't mean they're not important!

ADVERBS
*An adverb modifies a verb, an adjective, or another adverb and tells **how, where, when,** or **to what extent**.*

PRONOUNS
A pronoun takes the place of one or more nouns or pronouns.

PREPOSITIONS
A preposition shows a logical relationship or locates an object in time or space.

CONJUNCTIONS
A conjunction joins words or word groups.

INTERJECTIONS
An interjection expresses strong or mild emotion.

SECTION ONE: WORD PREVIEW
Welcome to your ten new favorite words!

When you encounter a new word, take a moment to consider what it might mean.

1. Think about the word and circle what part of speech you think it is. *(Many words can act as more than one part of speech, depending on how they're used in the sentence, **so only choose one part of speech below**.)*

2. Come up with a brief definition of the word in the part of speech you've chosen. It doesn't have to be the *correct* definition—just do your best.

viewpoint
Part of Speech: noun   verb   adjective

*Definition:*_____

ferocious
Part of Speech: noun   verb   adjective

*Definition:*_____

construct
Part of Speech: noun   verb   adjective

*Definition:*_____

repetition
Part of Speech: noun   verb   adjective

*Definition:*_____

manipulate
Part of Speech: noun   verb   adjective

*Definition:*_____

reinforce
Part of Speech: noun   verb   adjective

*Definition:*_____

unique
Part of Speech: noun   verb   adjective

*Definition:*_____

tentative
Part of Speech: noun   verb   adjective

*Definition:*_____

quote
Part of Speech: noun   verb   adjective

*Definition:*_____

anticipate
Part of Speech: noun   verb   adjective

*Definition:*_____

viewpoint

view·point • [vyOO-point] • \ ˈvyo͞o͝ˌpoint \

- **noun**

   1. a particular attitude or way of considering a matter;
   2. the position from which something or someone is observed

Rico and I don't agree about everything, but we do have the same **viewpoint** on chocolate: we both love it.

SYNONYMS

ANTONYMS

WRITING TIME!
Use *viewpoint* in an original sentence of your own creation.

BONUS FUN TIME!
Express *viewpoint* with a drawing, or
invent a dictionary-style definition of your own.

ferocious

fe·ro·cious   •   [fuhr-rOH-shuhs]   •   \ fəˈrōSHəs \

- adjective

1. savagely fierce, cruel, or violent

I always run away from the **ferocious** dog that lives down the street.

SYNONYMS

ANTONYMS

WRITING TIME!

Use *ferocious* in an original sentence of your own creation.

BONUS FUN TIME!

Express *ferocious* with a drawing, or
invent a dictionary-style definition of your own.

construct

con·struct • [kuhn-strUHkt] • \ kənˈstrəkt \

- verb

  1. to build or erect something;

  2. to form an idea or theory

The crow **constructed** an elaborate nest out of old plastic trash.

SYNONYMS

ANTONYMS

WRITING TIME!

Use *construct* in an original sentence of your own creation.

BONUS FUN TIME!

Express *construct* with a drawing, or
invent a dictionary-style definition of your own.

repetition

rep·e·ti·tion   •   [rep-uh-tIsh-uhn]   •   \ ˌrepəˈtiSH(ə)n \

- noun
>   *1. the action of repeating something;*
>   *2. the recurrence of an action or event*

You can only really get better at playing a new song on the piano with practice and **repetition**.

SYNONYMS

ANTONYMS

WRITING TIME!
Use *repetition* in an original sentence of your own creation.

BONUS FUN TIME!
Express *repetition* with a drawing, or
invent a dictionary-style definition of your own.

manipulate

ma·nip·u·late • [muh-nIp-yuh-layt] • \ məˈnipyəˌlāt \

- verb

1. to handle or control a tool, mechanism, etc.;

2. to influence a person or situation cleverly or unscrupulously

I **manipulated** the hanging claw in the arcade and made it grab a big pink stuffed bunny.

SYNONYMS

ANTONYMS

WRITING TIME!

Use *manipulate* in an original sentence of your own creation.

BONUS FUN TIME!

Express *manipulate* with a drawing, or
invent a dictionary-style definition of your own.

reinforce

re·in·force • [ree-uhn-fORs] • \ ˌrēinˈfôrs \

- verb

1. to strengthen or support (an object or substance), especially with additional material

We will **reinforce** this door by putting a couch in front of it so that nobody will be able to break in.

SYNONYMS

_____

_____

ANTONYMS

_____

_____

WRITING TIME!

Use *reinforce* in an original sentence of your own creation.

_____

_____

BONUS FUN TIME!

Express *reinforce* with a drawing, or
invent a dictionary-style definition of your own.

unique

u·nique   •   [yu-nEEk]   •   \ yōoˈnēk \

- adjective

    1. being the only one of its kind : unlike anything else;

    2. particularly remarkable, special, or unusual

Carson thought his baseball card was **unique**, but I've seen a bunch of cards just like it.

SYNONYMS

ANTONYMS

WRITING TIME!

Use *unique* in an original sentence of your own creation.

BONUS FUN TIME!

Express *unique* with a drawing, or
invent a dictionary-style definition of your own.

tentative

ten·ta·tive • [tEn-tuh-tiv] • \ ˈten(t)ədiv \

- adjective

1. not certain or fixed; provisional;

2. done without confidence; hesitant

These rules are only **tentative**, but we'll make permanent ones soon.

SYNONYMS

ANTONYMS

WRITING TIME!

Use *tentative* in an original sentence of your own creation.

BONUS FUN TIME!

Express *tentative* with a drawing, or
invent a dictionary-style definition of your own.

quote

quote • [kwOHt] • \ kwōt \

- verb
1. *to repeat a passage from an existing work or statement;*
2. *to give an estimated price of a job or service*

I **quoted** my favorite poem on my senior yearbook page.

SYNONYMS

ANTONYMS

WRITING TIME!
Use *quote* in an original sentence of your own creation.

BONUS FUN TIME!
Express *quote* with a drawing, or
invent a dictionary-style definition of your own.

anticipate

an·tic·i·pate • [an-tls-uh-payt] • \ anˈtisəˌpāt \

- verb
   1. to expect or predict;
   2. to regard as probable

Zeke **anticipated** the homework assignment, so he wasn't caught by surprise.

SYNONYMS

ANTONYMS

WRITING TIME!
Use *anticipate* in an original sentence of your own creation.

BONUS FUN TIME!
Express *anticipate* with a drawing, or
invent a dictionary-style definition of your own.

SECTION ONE: WORD REVIEW

Congratulations on learning ten amazing new words! Remember that the whole point of learning new vocabulary is actually to use it, so let's put your new vocabulary to use.

1. Review the words you've learned. Consider what ideas come to mind when you say the words. How about when you read the definitions?
2. Circle at least **two** of your favorites. You'll get to use these when you write your very own story!

viewpoint —— noun
1. a particular attitude or way of considering a matter;
2. the position from which something or someone is observed

ferocious —— adjective
1. savagely fierce, cruel, or violent

construct —— verb
1. to build or erect something;
2. to form an idea or theory

repetition —— noun
1. the action of repeating something;
2. the recurrence of an action or event

manipulate —— verb
1. to handle or control a tool, mechanism, etc.;
2. to influence a person or situation

reinforce —— verb
1. to strengthen or support (an object or substance), especially with additional material

unique —— adjective
1. being the only one of its kind : unlike anything else;
2. particularly remarkable, special, or

tentative —— verb
1. not certain or fixed; provisional;
2. done without confidence; hesitant

quote —— verb
1. to repeat a passage from an existing work or statement;
2. to give an estimated price of a job or service

anticipate —— verb
1. to expect or predict;
2. to regard as probable

Story One

1. List the words you've chosen:

_____

2. Write a story that incorporates all of your chosen words. If you can't think of anything to write about, consider these suggestions:
   - **Write a story in which the main character has a secret identity.**
   - **Write a story that starts with you winning the lottery.**

Title: _____

_____

_____

_____

_____

_____

_____

_____

_____

Wonderful Words for Sixth Grade Vocabulary & Writing Workbook ©2021 Grammaropolis LLC

Section Two: Word Preview
Welcome to your ten new favorite words!

When you encounter a new word, take a moment to consider what it might mean.

1. Think about the word and circle what part of speech you think it is.
   *(Many words can act as more than one part of speech, depending on how they're used in the sentence, **so only choose one part of speech below.**)*
2. Come up with a brief definition of the word in the part of speech you've chosen. It doesn't have to be the *correct* definition—just do your best.

elaborate
Part of Speech: noun   verb   adjective

Definition:_____

expression
Part of Speech: noun   verb   adjective

Definition:_____

encourage
Part of Speech: noun   verb   adjective

Definition:_____

frequency
Part of Speech: noun   verb   adjective

Definition:_____

adapt
Part of Speech: noun   verb   adjective

Definition:_____

unanimous
Part of Speech: noun   verb   adjective

Definition:_____

accumulate
Part of Speech: noun   verb   adjective

Definition:_____

continuous
Part of Speech: noun   verb   adjective

Definition:_____

origin
Part of Speech: noun   verb   adjective

Definition:_____

contribute
Part of Speech: noun   verb   adjective

Definition:_____

elaborate

e·lab·o·rate   •   [i-lAb-uhr-ruht]   •   \ əˈlabəˌrāt \

- verb

1. to develop or present (a theory, policy, or system) in detail;

2. to add more detail concerning what has already been said

I didn't understand what you meant by that, so could you please **elaborate** on the point you're trying to make?

SYNONYMS

ANTONYMS

WRITING TIME!

Use *elaborate* in an original sentence of your own creation.

BONUS FUN TIME!

Express *elaborate* with a drawing, or
invent a dictionary-style definition of your own.

expression

ex·pres·sion   •   [ik-sprEsh-uhn]   •   \ ikˈspreSHən \

- noun

    1. a look on someone's face that conveys a particular emotion;

    2. a word or phrase used to convey an idea

We snuck back home late last night and were met with an **expression** of pure disappointment on my mom's face.

SYNONYMS

ANTONYMS

WRITING TIME!

Use *expression* in an original sentence of your own creation.

BONUS FUN TIME!

Express *expression* with a drawing, or
invent a dictionary-style definition of your own.

encourage

en·cour·age • [in-kUHR-rij] • \ inˈkərij \

- **verb**

    1. to give support, confidence, or hope;

    2. to help develop or stimulate an activity, state, or view

The coach **encouraged** her players by reminding them how much they'd prepared for the game.

SYNONYMS

ANTONYMS

WRITING TIME!

Use *encourage* in an original sentence of your own creation.

BONUS FUN TIME!

Express *encourage* with a drawing, or
invent a dictionary-style definition of your own.

frequency

fre·quen·cy • [frEE-kwuhn-see] • \ ˈfrēkwənsē \

- noun

    1. the rate at which something occurs or is repeated over a particular period of time or in a given sample

We're not watering the lawn often enough, so we'll have to water it with greater **frequency**.

SYNONYMS

_____

_____

ANTONYMS

_____

_____

WRITING TIME!
Use *frequency* in an original sentence of your own creation.

_____

_____

_____

BONUS FUN TIME!
Express *frequency* with a drawing, or
invent a dictionary-style definition of your own.

adapt

a·dapt • [uh-dApt] • \ əˈdapt \

- verb

1. to make fit (as for a new use) often by modification

The car wasn't designed to go off-roading, but my aunt **adapted** it by giving it four-wheel drive.

SYNONYMS

ANTONYMS

WRITING TIME!
Use *adapt* in an original sentence of your own creation.

_____

_____

_____

BONUS FUN TIME!
Express *adapt* with a drawing, or
invent a dictionary-style definition of your own.

unanimous

u·nan·i·mous   •   [yoo-nAn-uh-muhs] •   \ yo͞oˈnanəməs \

- adjective

1. (of two or more people) fully in agreement

We took a vote, and the decision was **unanimous**; everyone agreed!

SYNONYMS

ANTONYMS

WRITING TIME!
Use *unanimous* in an original sentence of your own creation.

BONUS FUN TIME!
Express *unanimous* with a drawing, or
invent a dictionary-style definition of your own.

accumulate

ac·cu·mu·late • [uh-kyOO-myuh-layt] • \ əˈkyo͞om(y)əˌlāt \

- verb

> *1. to gather together or acquire an increasing number or quantity of*

My uncle **accumulated** an incredible gnome collection over almost fifty years.

SYNONYMS

ANTONYMS

WRITING TIME!
Use *accumulate* in an original sentence of your own creation.

BONUS FUN TIME!
Express *accumulate* with a drawing, or
invent a dictionary-style definition of your own.

continuous

con·tin·u·ous • [kuhn-tIn-yoo-uhs] • \ kənˈtinyo͞oəs \

- adjective

1. forming an unbroken whole;
2. without interruption

The sugar ants marched in a **continuous** line all the way across the kitchen counter.

SYNONYMS

ANTONYMS

WRITING TIME!

Use *continuous* in an original sentence of your own creation.

BONUS FUN TIME!

Express *continuous* with a drawing, or
invent a dictionary-style definition of your own.

origin

or·i·gin　　•　　[OR-uh-juhn]　　•　　\ ˈôrəjən \

- noun

1. the point or place where something begins, arises, or is derived

Do you happen to know the **origin** of the saying, "Wherever you go, there you are."?

SYNONYMS

ANTONYMS

WRITING TIME!

Use *origin* in an original sentence of your own creation.

BONUS FUN TIME!

Express *origin* with a drawing, or
invent a dictionary-style definition of your own.

contribute

con·trib·ute   •   [kuhn-trIb-yoot]   •   \ kənˈtribyo͞ot \

- verb

1. give something (money, time, etc.) in order to help achieve or provide something

If everyone **contributes** even a little bit of time and effort, I am sure that we can build this hiking trail quickly.

SYNONYMS

ANTONYMS

WRITING TIME!

Use *contribute* in an original sentence of your own creation.

BONUS FUN TIME!

Express *contribute* with a drawing, or
invent a dictionary-style definition of your own.

Section Two: Word Review

Congratulations on learning ten amazing new words! Remember that the whole point of learning new vocabulary is actually to use it, so let's put your new vocabulary to use.

1. Review the words you've learned. Consider what ideas come to mind when you say the words. How about when you read the definitions?
2. Circle at least **two** of your favorites. You'll get to use these when you write your very own story!

elaborate —— verb
1. to develop or present (a theory, policy, or system) in detail;
2. to add more detail concerning what has already been said

expression —— noun
1. a look on someone's face that conveys a particular emotion;
2. a word or phrase used to convey an idea

encourage —— verb
1. to give support, confidence, or hope;
2. to help develop or stimulate an activity, state, or view

frequency —— noun
1. the rate at which something occurs or is repeated over a particular period of time or in a given sample

adapt —— verb
1. to make fit (as for a new use) often by modification

unanimous —— adjective
1. (of two or more people) fully in agreement

accumulate —— verb
1. to gather together or acquire an increasing number or quantity of

continuous —— adjective
1. forming an unbroken whole;
2. without interruption

origin —— noun
1. the point or place where something begins, arises, or is derived

contribute —— verb
1. give something (money, time, etc.) i in order to help achieve or provide something

STORY TWO

1. List the words you've chosen:

_____

2. Write a story that incorporates all of your chosen words. If you can't think of anything to write about, consider these suggestions:

   - **Write a story that takes place in a small human settlement on Mars.**

   - **Write a story in which you wake up one morning as a talking dog.**

Title: _____

_____

_____

_____

_____

_____

_____

_____

_____

_____

_____

_____

_____

Wonderful Words for Sixth Grade Vocabulary & Writing Workbook ©2021 Grammaropolis LLC

SECTION THREE: WORD PREVIEW
Welcome to your ten new favorite words!

When you encounter a new word, take a moment to consider what it might mean.

1. Think about the word and circle what part of speech you think it is. *(Many words can act as more than one part of speech, depending on how they're used in the sentence, **so only choose one part of speech below**.)*
2. Come up with a brief definition of the word in the part of speech you've chosen. It doesn't have to be the *correct* definition—just do your best.

equation
Part of Speech: noun   verb   adjective

Definition:_____

factor
Part of Speech: noun   verb   adjective

Definition:_____

democracy
Part of Speech: noun   verb   adjective

Definition:_____

dimension
Part of Speech: noun   verb   adjective

Definition:_____

genuine
Part of Speech: noun   verb   adjective

Definition:_____

drastic
Part of Speech: noun   verb   adjective

Definition:_____

history
Part of Speech: noun   verb   adjective

Definition:_____

consequence
Part of Speech: noun   verb   adjective

Definition:_____

massive
Part of Speech: noun   verb   adjective

Definition:_____

civilization
Part of Speech: noun   verb   adjective

Definition:_____

equation

e·qua·tion • [i-kwAY-zhuhn] • \ əˈkwāZHən \

- noun

1. a statement of two mathematical expressions being equal;

2. a situation in which several factors must be taken into account

The **equation** seemed difficult until I remembered that two plus two was, in fact, four.

SYNONYMS

ANTONYMS

WRITING TIME!

Use *equation* in an original sentence of your own creation.

BONUS FUN TIME!

Express *equation* with a drawing, or
invent a dictionary-style definition of your own.

factor

fac·tor • [fAk-tuhr] • \ ˈfaktər \

- **noun**

 1. a circumstance, fact, or influence that contributes to a result or outcome

 I think the restaurant failed because their food was bad, but there could have been other **factors** that contributed to it.

SYNONYMS

ANTONYMS

WRITING TIME!
Use *factor* in an original sentence of your own creation.

BONUS FUN TIME!
Express *factor* with a drawing, or
invent a dictionary-style definition of your own.

democracy

de·moc·ra·cy • [di-mAHk-ruh-see] • \ dəˈmäkrəsē \

- noun

1. *a system of government by all the eligible members of a state, typically through elected representatives*

My mom always used to say, "This is not a **democracy**! I'm the parent, and I get to decide for all of us!"

SYNONYMS

ANTONYMS

WRITING TIME!
Use *democracy* in an original sentence of your own creation.

BONUS FUN TIME!
Express *democracy* with a drawing, or
invent a dictionary-style definition of your own.

dimension

di·men·sion • [duh-mEn-shuhn] • \ dəˈmen(t)SH(ə)n \

- noun

1. *a measurable extent of some kind;*
2. *an aspect or feature of a situation, problem, or thing*

There are many **dimensions** to this issue; one answer isn't going to address all of them.

SYNONYMS

ANTONYMS

WRITING TIME!

Use *dimension* in an original sentence of your own creation.

BONUS FUN TIME!

Express *dimension* with a drawing, or
invent a dictionary-style definition of your own.

genuine

gen·u·ine • [jEn-yuh-wuhn] • \ ˈjenyo͞oən \

- adjective

1. *truly what something is said to be : authentic;*
2. *(of a person, emotion, or action) sincere*

You may think it's a knock-off, but that's a **genuine** Rolex watch!

SYNONYMS

ANTONYMS

WRITING TIME!
Use *genuine* in an original sentence of your own creation.

BONUS FUN TIME!
Express *genuine* with a drawing, or
invent a dictionary-style definition of your own.

drastic

dras·tic   •   [drAs-tik]   •   \ ˈdrastik \

- **adjective**
  1. *likely to have a strong or far-reaching effect;*
  2. *radical and extreme*

We are going to have to take **drastic** steps if we're going to have any hope of lowering greenhouse gas emissions.

SYNONYMS

ANTONYMS

WRITING TIME!

Use *drastic* in an original sentence of your own creation.

BONUS FUN TIME!

Express *drastic* with a drawing, or
invent a dictionary-style definition of your own.

history

his·to·ry • [hIs-tuhr-ree] • \ ˈhist(ə)rē \

- noun

> 1. a series of past events connected with someone or something;
> 2. the study of past events, particularly in human affairs

If you knew the **history** of this school, you'd know why it's such a bad idea to dress up as a polar bear.

SYNONYMS

ANTONYMS

WRITING TIME!
Use *history* in an original sentence of your own creation.

BONUS FUN TIME!
Express *history* with a drawing, or
invent a dictionary-style definition of your own.

consequence

con·se·quence • [kAHn-suh-kwens] • \ ˈkänsikwəns \

> **- noun**
>
> *1. a result or effect of an action or condition*
>
> The **consequence** of my breaking the window was that I had to pull weeds for two weeks to earn enough money to pay for it.

SYNONYMS

ANTONYMS

WRITING TIME!
Use *consequence* in an original sentence of your own creation.

BONUS FUN TIME!
Express *consequence* with a drawing, or
invent a dictionary-style definition of your own.

massive

mas·sive • [mAs-iv] • \ ˈmasiv \

- **adjective**
    1. large and heavy or solid;
    2. exceptionally large

Stonehenge is basically a famous circle of **massive** rocks.

SYNONYMS

ANTONYMS

WRITING TIME!

Use *massive* in an original sentence of your own creation.

BONUS FUN TIME!

Express *massive* with a drawing, or
invent a dictionary-style definition of your own.

civilization

civ·i·li·za·tion • [siv-uh-luh-zAY-shuhn] • \ ˌsivələˈzāSH(ə)n \

- noun

    1. the society, culture, and way of life of a particular area;

    2. the comfort and convenience of modern life

The center of the Inca **civilization** was in the city of Cuzco, in modern-day Peru.

SYNONYMS

ANTONYMS

WRITING TIME!

Use *civilization* in an original sentence of your own creation.

BONUS FUN TIME!

Express *civilization* with a drawing, or
invent a dictionary-style definition of your own.

SECTION THREE: WORD REVIEW

Congratulations on learning ten amazing new words! Remember that the whole point of learning new vocabulary is actually to use it, so let's put your new vocabulary to use.

1. Review the words you've learned. Consider what ideas come to mind when you say the words. How about when you read the definitions?
2. Circle at least **two** of your favorites. You'll get to use these when you write your very own story!

equation — noun

1. *a statement of two mathematical expressions being equal;*
2. *a situation in which several factors must be taken into account*

factor — noun

1. *a circumstance, fact, or influence that contributes to a result or outcome*

democracy — noun

1. *a system of government by all the eligible members of a state, typically through elected representatives*

dimension — noun

1. *a measurable extent of some kind;*
2. *an aspect or feature of a situation, problem, or thing*

genuine — adjective

1. *truly what something is said to be : authentic;*
2. *(of a person, emotion, or action) sincere*

drastic — adjective

1. *likely to have a strong or far-reaching effect;*
2. *radical and extreme*

history — noun

1. *a series of past events connected with someone or something;*
2. *the study of past events, particularly in human affairs*

consequence — noun

1. *a result or effect of an action or condition*

massive — adjective

1. *large and heavy or solid;*
2. *exceptionally large*

civilization — noun

1. *the society, culture, and way of life of a particular area;*
2. *the comfort and convenience of modern life*

STORY THREE

1. List the words you've chosen:

_____

2. Write a story that incorporates all of your chosen words. If you can't think of anything to write about, consider these suggestions:
   - **Write a story that takes place on Halloween night.**
   - **Write a story in which you're an alien who lands on Earth and the first human you meet is your teacher.**

Title: _____

_____

_____

_____

_____

_____

_____

_____

_____

_____

_____

SECTION FOUR: WORD PREVIEW
Welcome to your ten new favorite words!

When you encounter a new word, take a moment to consider what it might mean.

1. Think about the word and circle what part of speech you think it is. *(Many words can act as more than one part of speech, depending on how they're used in the sentence, **so only choose one part of speech below**.)*

2. Come up with a brief definition of the word in the part of speech you've chosen. It doesn't have to be the *correct* definition—just do your best.

lofty
Part of Speech: noun   verb   adjective

Definition:_____

obedient
Part of Speech: noun   verb   adjective

Definition:_____

priority
Part of Speech: noun   verb   adjective

Definition:_____

catastrophe
Part of Speech: noun   verb   adjective

Definition:_____

persuade
Part of Speech: noun   verb   adjective

Definition:_____

suspense
Part of Speech: noun   verb   adjective

Definition:_____

exaggerate
Part of Speech: noun   verb   adjective

Definition:_____

conclusion
Part of Speech: noun   verb   adjective

Definition:_____

realistic
Part of Speech: noun   verb   adjective

Definition:_____

oblivious
Part of Speech: noun   verb   adjective

Definition:_____

lofty

loft·y • [lAWf-tee] • \ ˈlôftē \

- adjective

1. of imposing height;

2. of a noble or exalted nature

Kyle always sets **lofty** goals because he wants to accomplish a lot.

SYNONYMS

ANTONYMS

WRITING TIME!

Use *lofty* in an original sentence of your own creation.

BONUS FUN TIME!

Express *lofty* with a drawing, or
invent a dictionary-style definition of your own.

obedient

o·be·di·ent   •   [oh-bEE-dee-uhnt]   •   \ əˈbēdēənt \

- adjective

1. complying or willing to comply with orders or requests;

2. submissive to another's will

My grandpa says that I need to be more **obedient** and do what he tells me to do.

SYNONYMS

ANTONYMS

WRITING TIME!

Use *obedient* in an original sentence of your own creation.

BONUS FUN TIME!

Express *obedient* with a drawing, or
invent a dictionary-style definition of your own.

priority

pri·or·i·ty • [prie-AW-ruh-tee] • \ prīˈôrədē \

- noun

1. a thing that is regarded as more important than another

Because it's raining so hard right now, our **priority** should be to make sure that all of the car windows have been rolled up.

SYNONYMS

ANTONYMS

WRITING TIME!

Use *priority* in an original sentence of your own creation.

BONUS FUN TIME!

Express *priority* with a drawing, or invent a dictionary-style definition of your own.

catastrophe

ca·tas·tro·phe   •   [kuh-tA-struh-fee]   •   \ kəˈtastrəfē \

- noun

1. *an event causing great and often sudden damage or suffering;*
2. *a disaster*

The raging wildfire was a **catastrophe** for the people and animals in the nearby towns.

SYNONYMS

ANTONYMS

WRITING TIME!

Use *catastrophe* in an original sentence of your own creation.

BONUS FUN TIME!

Express *catastrophe* with a drawing, or
invent a dictionary-style definition of your own.

persuade

per·suade   •   [puhr-swAYd]   •   \ pərˈswād \

> **- verb**
>
> *1. to cause (someone) to do something through reasoning or argument : convince*
>
> Nayla **persuaded** her little brother to share his donut with her by reminding him that she shared with him last time.

Synonyms

Antonyms

Writing Time!
Use *persuade* in an original sentence of your own creation.

Bonus Fun Time!
Express *persuade* with a drawing, or
invent a dictionary-style definition of your own.

suspense

sus·pense   •   [suh-spEns]   •   \ səˈspens \

- noun

1. a state or feeling of excited or anxious uncertainty about what may happen

I begged Gerald to tell me where we were going to dinner, but he wanted to keep me in **suspense**, so he didn't tell me.

SYNONYMS

ANTONYMS

WRITING TIME!
Use *suspense* in an original sentence of your own creation.

BONUS FUN TIME!
Express *suspense* with a drawing, or
invent a dictionary-style definition of your own.

exaggerate

ex·ag·ger·ate • [ig-zAj-uhr-rayt] • \ igˈzajəˌrāt \

- verb

1. to represent (something) as being larger, better, or worse than it really is

Evelyn **exaggerates** all the time, so you can never tell if she is telling the truth or if she's trying to impress you.

SYNONYMS

ANTONYMS

WRITING TIME!
Use *exaggerate* in an original sentence of your own creation.

BONUS FUN TIME!
Express *exaggerate* with a drawing, or
invent a dictionary-style definition of your own.

conclusion

con·clu·sion   •   [kuhn-klOO-zhuhn]   •   \ kənˈklooZHən \

- **noun**

    1. the end or finish of an event or process;

    2. a judgment or decision reached by reasoning

At the **conclusion** of the big meeting, Dav's boss challenged him to do a better job.

SYNONYMS

ANTONYMS

WRITING TIME!

Use *conclusion* in an original sentence of your own creation.

BONUS FUN TIME!

Express *conclusion* with a drawing, or
invent a dictionary-style definition of your own.

realistic

re·al·is·tic　　•　　[ree-uh-lIs-tik]　　•　　\ ˌrēəˈlistik \

- adjective

　1. *showing a practical idea of what can be achieved or expected;*

　2. *representing things in a way that is accurate or true to life*

Video game technology is making the characters look more and more **realistic** every year.

SYNONYMS

ANTONYMS

WRITING TIME!

Use *realistic* in an original sentence of your own creation.

BONUS FUN TIME!

Express *realistic* with a drawing, or
invent a dictionary-style definition of your own.

oblivious

ob·liv·i·ous   •   [uh-blIv-ee-uhs]   •   \ əˈblivēəs \

- adjective

   1. not aware of or not concerned about what is happening around one

When Wendy told me she didn't know what our homework was, I couldn't believe how **oblivious** she was about school.

SYNONYMS

ANTONYMS

WRITING TIME!
Use *oblivious* in an original sentence of your own creation.

BONUS FUN TIME!
Express *oblivious* with a drawing, or
invent a dictionary-style definition of your own.

SECTION FOUR: WORD REVIEW

Congratulations on learning ten amazing new words! Remember that the whole point of learning new vocabulary is actually to use it, so let's put your new vocabulary to use.

1. Review the words you've learned. Consider what ideas come to mind when you say the words. How about when you read the definitions?
2. Circle at least **two** of your favorites. You'll get to use these when you write your very own story!

lofty —————— adjective
1. of imposing height;
2. of a noble or exalted nature

obedient —————— adjective
1. complying or willing to comply with orders or requests;
2. submissive to another's will

priority —————— noun
1. a thing that is regarded as more important than another

catastrophe —————— noun
1. an event causing great and often sudden damage or suffering;
2. a disaster

persuade —————— verb
1. to cause (someone) to do something through reasoning or argument : convince

suspense —————— noun
1. a state or feeling of excited or anxious uncertainty about what may happen

exaggerate —————— verb
1. to represent (something) as being larger, better, or worse than it really is

conclusion —————— noun
1. the end or finish of an event or process;
2. a judgment or decision reached by reasoning

realistic —————— adjective
1. showing a practical idea of what can be achieved or expected;
2. representing things in a way that is accurate or true to life

oblivious —————— adjective
1. not aware of or not concerned about what is happening around one

STORY FOUR

1. List the words you've chosen:

_____

2. Write a story that incorporates all of your chosen words. If you can't think of anything to write about, consider these suggestions:
   - **Write a story that begins with you finding a functional magic wand in the middle of the sidewalk.**
   - **Write a story that takes place in a restaurant parking lot.**

Title: _____

_____

_____

_____

_____

_____

_____

_____

_____

_____

_____

_____

_____

_____

Wonderful Words for Sixth Grade Vocabulary & Writing Workbook ©2021 Grammaropolis LLC

SECTION FIVE: WORD PREVIEW
Welcome to your ten new favorite words!

When you encounter a new word, take a moment to consider what it might mean.

1. Think about the word and circle what part of speech you think it is. *(Many words can act as more than one part of speech, depending on how they're used in the sentence, **so only choose one part of speech below.**)*
2. Come up with a brief definition of the word in the part of speech you've chosen. It doesn't have to be the *correct* definition—just do your best.

chronological
Part of Speech: noun   verb   adjective

*Definition:*_____
_____

insist
Part of Speech: noun   verb   adjective

*Definition:*_____
_____

retrieve
Part of Speech: noun   verb   adjective

*Definition:*_____
_____

congruent
Part of Speech: noun   verb   adjective

*Definition:*_____
_____

declare
Part of Speech: noun   verb   adjective

*Definition:*_____
_____

artifact
Part of Speech: noun   verb   adjective

*Definition:*_____
_____

narrate
Part of Speech: noun   verb   adjective

*Definition:*_____
_____

strategic
Part of Speech: noun   verb   adjective

*Definition:*_____
_____

violate
Part of Speech: noun   verb   adjective

*Definition:*_____
_____

adequate
Part of Speech: noun   verb   adjective

*Definition:*_____
_____

chronological

chron·o·log·i·cal • [krahn-uh-lAHj-i-kuhl] • \ ˌkränəˈläjək(ə)l \

- adjective

1. (of a record of events) starting with the earliest and following the order in which they occurred

I like to organize my books in **chronological** order by publication date, but Ezra prefers to organize his books alphabetically.

SYNONYMS

ANTONYMS

WRITING TIME!
Use *chronological* in an original sentence of your own creation.

BONUS FUN TIME!
Express *chronological* with a drawing, or
invent a dictionary-style definition of your own.

insist

in·sist • [in-sIst] • \ inˈsist \

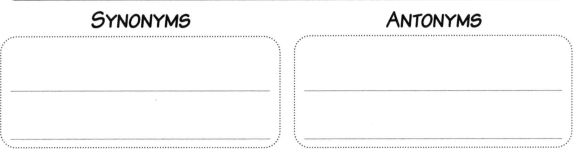

- verb

1. to demand something forcefully, not accepting refusal

Gbemi's grandmother **insisted** that I eat a second piece of cake, so I had to do it.

SYNONYMS

ANTONYMS

WRITING TIME!
Use *insist* in an original sentence of your own creation.

BONUS FUN TIME!
Express *insist* with a drawing, or
invent a dictionary-style definition of your own.

retrieve

re·trieve   •   [ri-trEEv]   •   \ rəˈtrēv \

- verb

1. to get or bring (something) back : regain possession of

I forgot my wallet at the movie theater, so we had to go back and **retrieve** it.

SYNONYMS

ANTONYMS

WRITING TIME!
Use *retrieve* in an original sentence of your own creation.

BONUS FUN TIME!
Express *retrieve* with a drawing, or
invent a dictionary-style definition of your own.

congruent

con·gru·ent • [kuhn-grOO-uhnt] • \ kənˈgrooənt \

- adjective

1. in agreement or harmony

It's important to find at least one friend whose idea of fun is **congruent** with yours.

SYNONYMS

ANTONYMS

WRITING TIME!

Use *congruent* in an original sentence of your own creation.

BONUS FUN TIME!

Express *congruent* with a drawing, or
invent a dictionary-style definition of your own.

declare

de·clare • [di-klAIR] • \ diˈkler \

- **verb**

1. *to say something in a solemn and emphatic manner;*
2. *to acknowledge possession of (income or goods)*

The mayor just **declared** that today is officially Good Grammar Day.

SYNONYMS

_____

_____

ANTONYMS

_____

_____

WRITING TIME!

Use *declare* in an original sentence of your own creation.

_____

_____

BONUS FUN TIME!

Express *declare* with a drawing, or
invent a dictionary-style definition of your own.

artifact

ar·ti·fact • [AHR-ti-fakt] • \ ˈärdəfakt \

- noun

1. an object made by a human being, typically an item of cultural or historical interest

We buried a time capsule so that future civilizations would be able to learn about us by studying the **artifacts** inside.

SYNONYMS

ANTONYMS

WRITING TIME!
Use *artifact* in an original sentence of your own creation.

BONUS FUN TIME!
Express *artifact* with a drawing, or
invent a dictionary-style definition of your own.

narrate

nar·rate   •   [nAIR-ayt]   •   \ ˈnerˌāt \

- verb

1. to give a spoken or written account of

We all sat around the fire while our counselor **narrated** fascinating stories from her childhood.

SYNONYMS

ANTONYMS

WRITING TIME!
Use *narrate* in an original sentence of your own creation.

BONUS FUN TIME!
Express *narrate* with a drawing, or
invent a dictionary-style definition of your own.

strategic

stra·te·gic • [strat-EE-jik] • \ strəˈtējik \

- adjective

1. relating to the identification of long-term or overall aims and interests and the means of achieving them

It's important to develop a **strategic** plan rather than just jumping into a situation and doing whatever comes to mind.

SYNONYMS

ANTONYMS

WRITING TIME!
Use *strategic* in an original sentence of your own creation.

BONUS FUN TIME!
Express *strategic* with a drawing, or
invent a dictionary-style definition of your own.

violate

vi·o·late   •   [vIE-uh-layt]   •   \ ˈvīəˌlāt \

- verb

    1. to break or fail to comply with (a rule or formal agreement);

    2. to fail to respect (someone's peace, privacy, or rights)

If you **violate** the seatbelt law by not putting on a seatbelt, you're going to get a ticket.

SYNONYMS

ANTONYMS

WRITING TIME!

Use *violate* in an original sentence of your own creation.

BONUS FUN TIME!

Express *violate* with a drawing, or
invent a dictionary-style definition of your own.

adequate

ad·e·quate • [Ad-i-kwuht] • \ ˈadəkwət \

- adjective

1. satisfactory or acceptable in quality or quantity

I tried to tell my parents that my allowance wasn't **adequate** for my needs, but they assured me that it was enough.

SYNONYMS

ANTONYMS

WRITING TIME!
Use *adequate* in an original sentence of your own creation.

BONUS FUN TIME!
Express *adequate* with a drawing, or
invent a dictionary-style definition of your own.

SECTION FIVE: WORD REVIEW

Congratulations on learning ten amazing new words! Remember that the whole point of learning new vocabulary is actually to use it, so let's put your new vocabulary to use.

1. Review the words you've learned. Consider what ideas come to mind when you say the words. How about when you read the definitions?
2. Circle at least **two** of your favorites. You'll get to use these when you write your very own story!

chronological – adjective

1. *(of a record of events) starting with the earliest and following the order in which they occurred*

insist — verb

1. *to demand something forcefully, not accepting refusal*

retrieve — verb

1. *to get or bring (something) back : regain possession of*

congruent — adjective

1. *in agreement or harmony*

declare — verb

1. *to say something in a solemn and emphatic manner;*
2. *to acknowledge possession of (income or goods)*

artifact — noun

1. *an object made by a human being, typically an item of cultural or historical interest*

narrate — verb

1. *to give a spoken or written account of*

strategic — adjective

1. *relating to the identification of long-term or overall aims and interests and the means of achieving them*

violate — verb

1. *to break or fail to comply with (a rule or formal agreement);*
2. *to fail to respect (someone's peace, privacy, or rights)*

adequate — adjective

1. *satisfactory or acceptable in quality or quantity*

STORY FIVE

1. List the words you've chosen:

_____

2. Write a story that incorporates all of your chosen words. If you can't think of anything to write about, consider these suggestions:
   - **Write a story in which the first sentence includes the words** *pineapple* **and** *surprise.*
   - **Write a story that takes place on a hot air balloon.**

Title: _____

_____

_____

_____

_____

_____

_____

_____

_____

_____

_____

_____

_____

_____

Wonderful Words for Sixth Grade Vocabulary & Writing Workbook ©2021 Grammaropolis LLC

SECTION SIX: WORD PREVIEW
Welcome to your ten new favorite words!

When you encounter a new word, take a moment to consider what it might mean.

1. Think about the word and circle what part of speech you think it is.
   (Many words can act as more than one part of speech, depending on how they're used in the sentence, **so only choose one part of speech below.**)
2. Come up with a brief definition of the word in the part of speech you've chosen. It doesn't have to be the *correct* definition—just do your best.

evaluate
Part of Speech: noun   verb   adjective

Definition:_____

transfer
Part of Speech: noun   verb   adjective

Definition:_____

solution
Part of Speech: noun   verb   adjective

Definition:_____

substitute
Part of Speech: noun   verb   adjective

Definition:_____

analyze
Part of Speech: noun   verb   adjective

Definition:_____

hypothesis
Part of Speech: noun   verb   adjective

Definition:_____

extend
Part of Speech: noun   verb   adjective

Definition:_____

similar
Part of Speech: noun   verb   adjective

Definition:_____

adjacent
Part of Speech: noun   verb   adjective

Definition:_____

citizen
Part of Speech: noun   verb   adjective

Definition:_____

evaluate

e·val·u·ate • [i-vAl-yuh-wayt] • \ əˈvalyəˌwāt \

- verb

1. to form an idea of the amount, number, or value of : assess

At the end of the year, the teacher **evaluated** his students by giving them a long essay to write.

SYNONYMS

ANTONYMS

WRITING TIME!
Use *evaluate* in an original sentence of your own creation.

BONUS FUN TIME!
Express *evaluate* with a drawing, or
invent a dictionary-style definition of your own.

transfer

trans·fer   •   [trAns-fuhr]   •   \ transˈfər \

- verb
> 1. *to move from one place to another;*
> 2. *to make over the possession of to someone else*

I **transferred** ownership of my Power Ranger collection to my little brother when I left for college.

SYNONYMS

ANTONYMS

WRITING TIME!
Use *transfer* in an original sentence of your own creation.

BONUS FUN TIME!
Express *transfer* with a drawing, or
invent a dictionary-style definition of your own.

solution

so·lu·tion • [suh-lOO-shuhn] • \ sə'lōōSH(ə)n \

- noun

    1. a means of solving a problem;

    2. a liquid mixture between a solute and a solvent

I know that if we work hard enough, we will be able to find the **solution** to this problem.

SYNONYMS

ANTONYMS

WRITING TIME!

Use *solution* in an original sentence of your own creation.

BONUS FUN TIME!

Express *solution* with a drawing, or
invent a dictionary-style definition of your own.

substitute

sub·sti·tute   •   [sUHb-stuh-toot]   •   \ ˈsəbstəˌt(y)o͞ot \

- verb

   1. to use or add in place of;

   2. to act or serve as a substitute

If you don't have vegetable oil for pancakes, just **substitute** it with melted butter.

SYNONYMS

ANTONYMS

WRITING TIME!
Use *substitute* in an original sentence of your own creation.

BONUS FUN TIME!
Express *substitute* with a drawing, or
invent a dictionary-style definition of your own.

analyze

an·a·lyze   •   [An-uh-liez]   •   \ ˈanlˌīz \

- verb

    1. to discover or reveal (something) through detailed examination

The scientist put the sample underneath a microscope so that she could **analyze** it more carefully.

SYNONYMS

ANTONYMS

WRITING TIME!
Use *analyze* in an original sentence of your own creation.

_____

_____

_____

BONUS FUN TIME!
Express *analyze* with a drawing, or
invent a dictionary-style definition of your own.

hypothesis

hy·poth·e·sis • [hie-pAHth-uh-suhs] • \ hīˈpäTHəsəs\

- noun

1. a supposition or proposed explanation made on the basis of limited evidence as a starting point for further investigation

My **hypothesis** is that I will be able to eat all of the donuts in this box, so let's find out if I'm right!

SYNONYMS

ANTONYMS

WRITING TIME!

Use *hypothesis* in an original sentence of your own creation.

BONUS FUN TIME!

Express *hypothesis* with a drawing, or
invent a dictionary-style definition of your own.

extend

ex·tend   •   [ik-stEnd]   •   \ ik'stend \

- verb

1. to cause to cover a larger area : make longer or wider;

2. to hold (something) out toward someone

Pretty soon, the city will **extend** all the way to the foot of that mountain over there.

SYNONYMS

ANTONYMS

WRITING TIME!
Use *extend* in an original sentence of your own creation.

BONUS FUN TIME!
Express *extend* with a drawing, or
invent a dictionary-style definition of your own.

similar

sim·i·lar   •   [sIm-uh-luhr]   •   \ ˈsim(ə)lər \

- adjective

1. resembling without being identical

People think my little brother and I are twins because we often have **similar** facial expressions.

SYNONYMS

ANTONYMS

WRITING TIME!

Use *similar* in an original sentence of your own creation.

BONUS FUN TIME!

Express *similar* with a drawing, or
invent a dictionary-style definition of your own.

adjacent

ad·ja·cent • [uh-jAY-s-nt] • \ əˈjās(ə)nt \

- adjective

1. next to or adjoining something else

It would be a great idea to build a smoothie shop **adjacent** to a high school because high school kids love smoothies.

SYNONYMS

ANTONYMS

WRITING TIME!

Use *adjacent* in an original sentence of your own creation.

BONUS FUN TIME!

Express *adjacent* with a drawing, or
invent a dictionary-style definition of your own.

citizen

cit·i·zen   •   [sIt-uh-zuhn]   •   \ ˈsidizən \

- noun

1. *a legally recognized subject of a state or commonwealth;*
2. *an inhabitant of a particular town or city*

If you want to be a **citizen** of Grammaropolis, all you have to do is have fun learning grammar.

SYNONYMS

ANTONYMS

WRITING TIME!

Use *citizen* in an original sentence of your own creation.

BONUS FUN TIME!

Express *citizen* with a drawing, or
invent a dictionary-style definition of your own.

SECTION SIX: WORD REVIEW

Congratulations on learning ten amazing new words! Remember that the whole point of learning new vocabulary is actually to use it, so let's put your new vocabulary to use.

1. Review the words you've learned. Consider what ideas come to mind when you say the words. How about when you read the definitions?
2. Circle at least **two** of your favorites. You'll get to use these when you write your very own story!

evaluate ———— verb

1. *to form an idea of the amount, number, or value of : assess*

transfer ———— verb

1. *to move from one place to another;*
2. *to make over the possession of to someone else*

solution ———— noun

1. *a means of solving a problem;*
2. *a liquid mixture between a solute and a solvent*

substitute ———— verb

1. *to use or add in place of;*
2. *to act or serve as a substitute*

analyze ———— verb

1. *to discover or reveal (something) through detailed examination*

hypothesis ———— noun

1. *a supposition or proposed explanation made on the basis of limited evidence as a starting point f or further investigation*

extend ———— verb

1. *to cause to cover a larger area : make longer or wider;*
2. *to hold (something) out toward someone*

similar ———— adjective

1. *resembling without being identical*

adjacent ———— adjective

1. *next to or adjoining something else*

citizen ———— noun

1. *a legally recognized subject of a state or commonwealth;*
2. *an inhabitant of a particular town or city*

Story Six

1. List the words you've chosen:

_____

2. Write a story that incorporates all of your chosen words. If you can't think of anything to write about, consider these suggestions:
   - **Write a story that starts with you jumping out of an airplane.**
   - **Write a story in which your main character runs a car dealership that is also the secret headquarters of a spy ring.**

Title: _____

_____

_____

_____

_____

_____

_____

_____

_____

_____

_____

_____

_____

_____

_____

_____

Wonderful Words for Sixth Grade Vocabulary & Writing Workbook ©2021 Grammaropolis LLC